Jr. Graphic Biographies™

Abraham Lincoln

and the Civil War

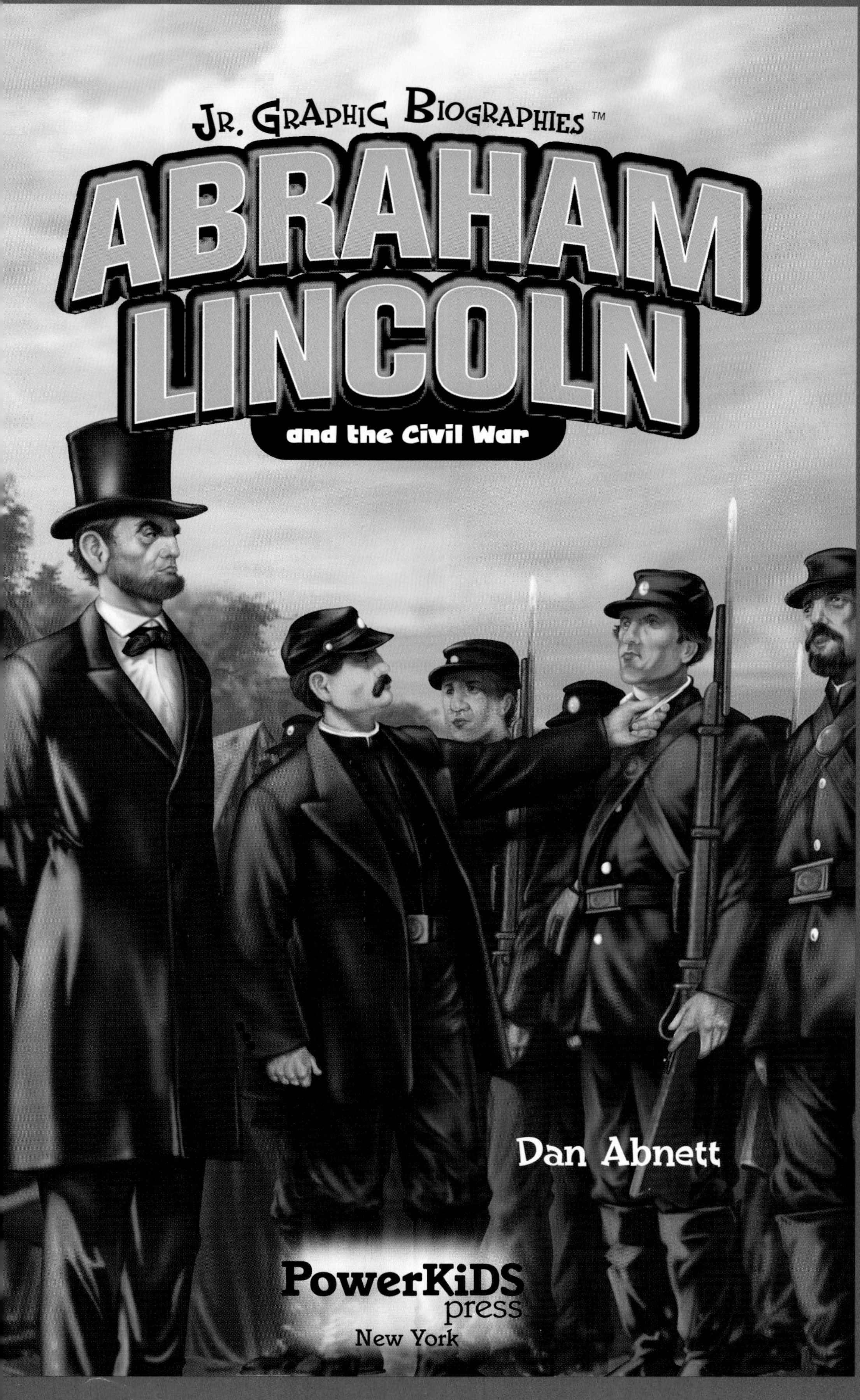

Dan Abnett

PowerKiDS press
New York

Published in 2007 by The Rosen Publishing Group, Inc.
29 East 21st Street, New York, NY 10010

First Edition

Editors: Joanne Randolph
Book Design: Julio Gil
Illustrations: Q2A

Library of Congress Cataloging-in-Publication Data

Abnett, Dan.
    Abraham Lincoln and the Civil War / Dan Abnett.— 1st ed.
        p. cm. — (Jr. graphic biographies)
    Includes index.
    ISBN (10) 1-4042-3392-X (13) 978-1-4042-3392-8 (lib. bdg.) —
ISBN (10) 1-4042-2145-X (13) 978-1-4042-2145-1 (pbk.)
    1. Lincoln, Abraham, 1809–1865—Juvenile literature. 2. Presidents—United States—Biography—Juvenile literature. 3. United States—History—Civil War, 1861–1865—Juvenile literature. I. Title. II. Series.
    E457.905.A26 2007
    973.7092—dc22

                                    2005037160

Manufactured in the United States of America

CONTENTS

MAIN CHARACTERS

 Abraham Lincoln (1809–1865) Sixteenth president of the United States and commander in chief of the **Union** army during the **Civil War**. Lincoln was an **opponent** of slavery, one of the causes of the Civil War.

 George McClellan (1826–1885) Commander of the main U.S. army in the early part of the war. Lincoln thought McClellan was too careful and did not want to fight a major battle.

 Mary Todd Lincoln (1818–1882) Married Abraham Lincoln in 1842. The deaths of her husband and three children caused her to become very sad.

 Jefferson Davis (1808–1889) President of the Confederate States of America during the Civil War. Before the war he was a hero in the U.S. army during the Mexican-American War.

 Robert E. Lee (1807-1870) Commander of the Confederate army, Lee was able to win many important battles against the larger and better-supplied Union army.

ABRAHAM LINCOLN AND THE CIVIL WAR

THE AMERICAN CIVIL WAR BEGAN IN 1861. AT THAT TIME, THE UNITED STATES WAS **DIVIDED** INTO TWO MAIN PARTS. THEY WERE THE NORTH, OR UNION STATES, AND THE SOUTH, OR CONFEDERATE STATES.

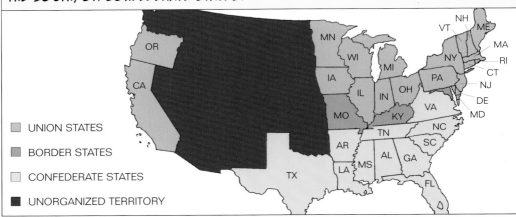

- UNION STATES
- BORDER STATES
- CONFEDERATE STATES
- UNORGANIZED TERRITORY

THE **ECONOMY** OF THE SOUTH WAS BASED ON FARMING. SLAVES WERE USED TO GROW CROPS SUCH AS COTTON AND **TOBACCO**.

THE ECONOMY OF THE NORTH WAS BASED ON **INDUSTRY** AND MANUFACTURING. SLAVERY WAS AGAINST THE LAW.

SLAVERY WOULD BECOME A CAUSE OF THE CIVIL WAR. IT WOULD ALSO PLAY AN IMPORTANT PART IN ABRAHAM LINCOLN'S LIFE.

ABRAHAM LINCOLN WAS BORN IN HARDIN COUNTY, KENTUCKY, ON FEBRUARY 12, 1809.

HE WORKED HARD. HE ALSO LOVED TO READ AND LEARN.

IN 1834, LINCOLN BEGAN TO WORK IN POLITICS.

HE MADE MANY SPEECHES AGAINST SLAVERY.

IN 1850, THE LINCOLNS' YOUNGEST SON, EDWARD, DIED. THIS WAS A SAD TIME FOR THE FAMILY.

IN 1860, THE REPUBLICAN PARTY CHOSE LINCOLN TO RUN FOR PRESIDENT OF THE UNITED STATES.

LINCOLN WAS ELECTED PRESIDENT IN NOVEMBER 1860.

THE PEOPLE IN THE SOUTH WERE NOT HAPPY. THEY THOUGHT LINCOLN WOULD TRY TO END SLAVERY.

BY FEBRUARY 1861, SOUTHERN STATES BEGAN TO WITHDRAW FROM THE UNION. THEY FORMED THE CONFEDERATE STATES OF AMERICA.

THEY ELECTED JEFFERSON DAVIS AS THEIR PRESIDENT.

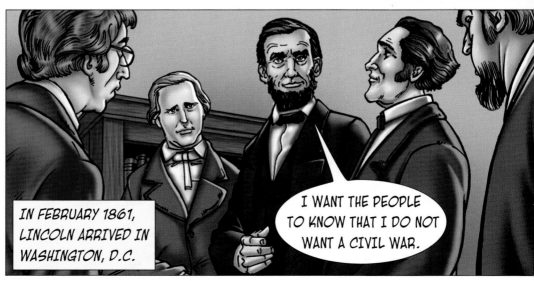

IN FEBRUARY 1861, LINCOLN ARRIVED IN WASHINGTON, D.C.

I WANT THE PEOPLE TO KNOW THAT I DO NOT WANT A CIVIL WAR.

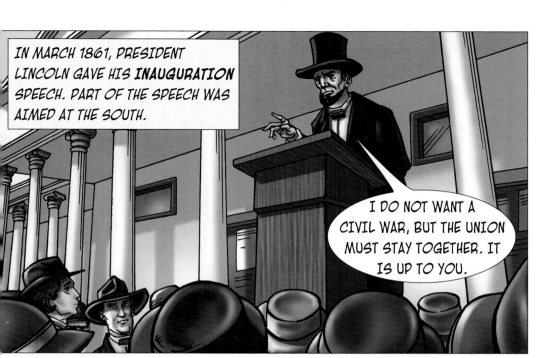

IN MARCH 1861, PRESIDENT LINCOLN GAVE HIS **INAUGURATION** SPEECH. PART OF THE SPEECH WAS AIMED AT THE SOUTH.

I DO NOT WANT A CIVIL WAR, BUT THE UNION MUST STAY TOGETHER. IT IS UP TO YOU.

IN HIS SPEECH LINCOLN ALSO SAID THAT THE U.S. GOVERNMENT WOULD KEEP CONTROL OF ALL ITS PROPERTY IN THE SOUTH.

ONE OF THOSE PLACES WAS FORT SUMTER IN CHARLESTON HARBOR, SOUTH CAROLINA.

ON APRIL 12, 1861, CONFEDERATE FORCES ATTACKED FORT SUMTER. THE CIVIL WAR HAD BEGUN.

PRESIDENT LINCOLN CALLED FOR 75,000 MEN TO FIGHT AGAINST THE SOUTH'S **REBELLION**.

SOUTHERN LEADER JEFFERSON DAVIS **ENLISTED** 100,000 MEN. MANY SOUTHERN OFFICERS HAD ONCE SERVED IN THE U.S. ARMY.

THE CONFEDERATE CAPITAL WAS IN RICHMOND, VIRGINIA.

THIS WAS ONLY 100 MILES (161 KM) FROM THE UNION CAPITAL IN WASHINGTON, D.C.

LINCOLN FEARED THE CITY WOULD BE ATTACKED.

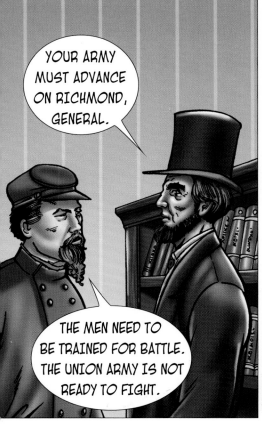

YOUR ARMY MUST ADVANCE ON RICHMOND, GENERAL.

THE MEN NEED TO BE TRAINED FOR BATTLE. THE UNION ARMY IS NOT READY TO FIGHT.

IF WE **DEFEAT** THE CONFEDERATE ARMY IN THEIR CAPITAL CITY, THE WAR WILL BE OVER QUICKLY.

FINALLY ON JULY 21, 1861, THE TWO ARMIES FOUGHT THE FIRST MAJOR BATTLE OF THE WAR. IT WAS THE FIRST BATTLE OF BULL RUN, FOUGHT IN VIRGINIA.

AT THE BEGINNING OF THE BATTLE, THE UNION ARMY SEEMED TO BE WINNING.

CONFEDERATE GENERALS THOMAS JACKSON AND BARNARD BEE FOUGHT SIDE BY SIDE.

GENERAL JACKSON, THEY ARE BEATING US BACK!

FORM UP, FORM UP! THERE STANDS JACKSON LIKE A STONE WALL.

SEEING THEIR BOLD LEADER, THE CONFEDERATE TROOPS BRAVELY RETURNED TO THE FIGHT.

FROM THEN ON GENERAL THOMAS JACKSON WAS KNOWN AS STONEWALL.

JACKSON HAD HELPED THE CONFEDERATES WIN THE WAR'S FIRST BATTLE.

AT THE WHITE HOUSE, IN WASHINGTON, D.C., PRESIDENT LINCOLN HEARD THE NEWS OF THE UNION DEFEAT.

WE MUST MAKE SOME CHANGES IF WE WANT TO WIN THIS WAR.

LINCOLN NAMED A NEW LEADER OF THE UNION FORCES.

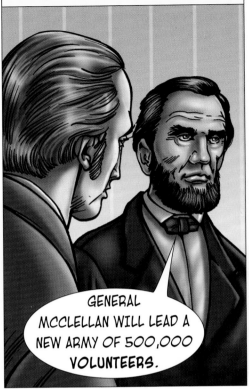

GENERAL MCCLELLAN WILL LEAD A NEW ARMY OF 500,000 VOLUNTEERS.

PRESIDENT LINCOLN ALSO APPOINTED EDWIN STANTON AS SECRETARY OF WAR IN 1862. TOGETHER HE AND LINCOLN BUILT A LARGE, WELL-TRAINED ARMY.

HOWEVER, LINCOLN'S NEW COMMANDER, GENERAL MCCLELLAN, DID NOT MOVE HIS ARMY INTO BATTLE QUICKLY.

MEANWHILE PRESIDENT LINCOLN SUFFERED MORE SADNESS.

THERE, THERE, MARY.

ANOTHER SON, 11-YEAR-OLD WILLIE, DIED.

WEEKS LATER PRESIDENT LINCOLN MET WITH SECRETARY STANTON.

OUR GENERAL GRANT IS FIGHTING AND WINNING IN THE WEST, BUT MCCLELLAN STILL WILL NOT FIGHT AT ALL!

MCCLELLAN IS AFRAID OF THE ENEMY. HE MUST ACT!

IN MARCH 1862, LINCOLN DEMOTED MCCLELLAN.

ON APRIL 7, 1862, UNION GENERAL ULYSSES S. GRANT WON A VERY IMPORTANT BATTLE AT SHILOH, TENNESSEE.

MCCLELLAN FINALLY ATTACKED YORKTOWN, AND THE CONFEDERATES HAVE LEFT.

IF ONLY MCCLELLAN COULD BE MORE LIKE GRANT.

GRANT LOST FAR TOO MANY MEN AT SHILOH, SIR.

I KNOW THE LOSSES ARE HEAVY, BUT GENERAL GRANT WINS BATTLES.

TAKE THIS TO THE PRESIDENT. BEFORE I CAN ATTACK RICHMOND, I NEED MORE MEN.

IN WASHINGTON LINCOLN READ MCCLELLAN'S NOTE.

HE ASKS FOR A BIGGER ARMY BUT DOES NOT FIGHT!

UNION SOLDIERS REMAINED CAMPED OUTSIDE RICHMOND FOR ONE MONTH.

MANY GOT SICK AND DIED, WITHOUT EVEN FIGHTING.

CONFEDERATE PRESIDENT DAVIS MET WITH HIS GENERAL, ROBERT E. LEE.

IF WE LOSE RICHMOND, WHAT SHOULD WE GUARD NEXT?

SIR, WE WILL NOT LOSE RICHMOND. WE MUST GUARD THE CITY!

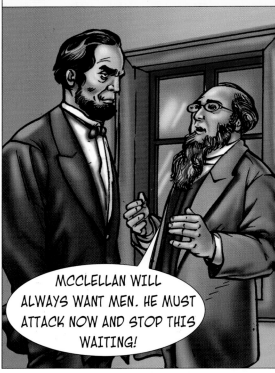

BACK AT THE WHITE HOUSE, LINCOLN AND STANTON TALKED ABOUT WHAT TO DO.

MCCLELLAN WILL ALWAYS WANT MEN. HE MUST ATTACK NOW AND STOP THIS WAITING!

FINALLY THE FIGHTING BEGAN.

THE TWO ARMIES FOUGHT FIVE BATTLES CLOSE TO RICHMOND.

MCCLELLAN WON SOME OF THE BATTLES AROUND RICHMOND. HOWEVER, HE WAS FORCED TO **RETREAT**.

GENERAL LEE IS THROWING EVERYTHING AT US. WE CANNOT WIN AT RICHMOND.

A YEAR HAS PASSED AND NOTHING HAS CHANGED.

LINCOLN WAS TIRED. HE WANTED THE WAR TO END.

IN SEPTEMBER 1862, IN MARYLAND, GENERAL LEE WAS PLANNING HIS NEXT MAJOR ATTACK.

ON SEPTEMBER 17, 1862, THE TWO ARMIES MET AT ANTIETAM CREEK IN SHARPSBURG, MARYLAND. THIS WAS THE BLOODIEST DAY OF BATTLE EVER FOUGHT ON AMERICAN SOIL.

THERE WERE ABOUT 26,000 MEN KILLED, WOUNDED, LOST, OR CAPTURED ON BOTH SIDES.

SO MANY MEN HAVE DIED FOR NOTHING. WE HAVE NOT WON THE BATTLE OF ANTIETAM.

THOUGH NEITHER SIDE HAD REALLY WON THE BATTLE, MOST NORTHERNERS SAW THE BATTLE OF ANTIETAM AS AN IMPORTANT **VICTORY** FOR THE UNION.

PRESIDENT LINCOLN SAW IT AS A TIME TO SET PEOPLE FREE.

NOW IS THE TIME FOR ME TO TELL THE PEOPLE WHAT I BELIEVE.

I BELIEVE IN A UNITED STATES OF AMERICA.

ABOVE ALL, I BELIEVE THAT ALL MEN WERE CREATED EQUAL.

IN SEPTEMBER 1862, LINCOLN MADE THE **EMANCIPATION PROCLAMATION.**

ALL PEOPLE HELD AS SLAVES IN THE CONFEDERATE STATES SHALL BE FOREVER FREE.

THE CIVIL WAR WENT ON.

IN 1864, LINCOLN WAS ELECTED TO A SECOND TERM OF OFFICE.

FINALLY THE CONFEDERATE GOVERNMENT **SURRENDERED** IN APRIL 1865, WHEN IT WAS CLEAR THEY WOULD NOT WIN. THE WAR WAS OVER.

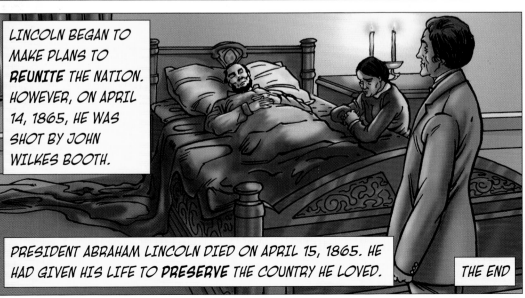

LINCOLN BEGAN TO MAKE PLANS TO **REUNITE** THE NATION. HOWEVER, ON APRIL 14, 1865, HE WAS SHOT BY JOHN WILKES BOOTH.

PRESIDENT ABRAHAM LINCOLN DIED ON APRIL 15, 1865. HE HAD GIVEN HIS LIFE TO **PRESERVE** THE COUNTRY HE LOVED.

THE END

TIMELINE

1809	On February 12, Abraham Lincoln is born in Hardin County, Kentucky.
1834	Lincoln is elected to the Illinois state government.
1842	Lincoln marries Mary Todd.
1846	He is elected to the U.S. House of Representatives.
1850	The Lincolns' youngest son, Edward, dies.
1860	Lincoln is elected president of the United States.
1861	He gives his first inauguration speech.
	Southern states leave the Union.
	Fort Sumter is attacked by Confederate forces.
	The First Battle of Bull Run is fought.
1862	The Lincolns' son Willie dies.
	The battles of Shiloh and Antietam are fought.
	Lincoln issues the Emancipation Proclamation.
1863	Lincoln gives the Gettysburg Address.
1865	The Confederate States of America surrenders to the Union.
	Lincoln is shot by John Wilkes Booth on April 14.
	President Abraham Lincoln dies on April 15.

GLOSSARY

Civil War (SIH-vul WOR) The war fought between the Northern and the Southern states of America from 1861 to 1865.

defeat (dih-FEET) To win against someone in a game or battle.

demoted (dih-MOHT-ed) To have lowered the rank of an officer.

divided (dih-VYD-ed) Broken apart or separated.

economy (ih-KAH-nuh-mee) The way in which a country or a business oversees its supplies and power sources.

Emancipation Proclamation (ih-man-sih-PAY-shun prak-luh-MAY-shun) A paper, signed by Abraham Lincoln during the Civil War, that freed all slaves held in Southern territory.

enlisted (en-LIST-ed) Got people to join the armed forces.

inauguration (ih-naw-gyuh-RAY-shun) The event of swearing in a government official.

industry (IN-dus-tree) A business in which many people work and make money producing a product.

opponent (uh-POH-nent) A person or a group that is against another.

preserve (prih-ZURV) To keep something from being lost or from going bad.

rebellion (rih-BEL-yun) A fight against one's government.

retreat (rih-TREET) To back away from a fight or another hard position.

reunite (ree-yoo-NYT) To join together again after being apart.

surrendered (suh-REN-derd) Gave up.

tobacco (tuh-BA-koh) A plant used for smoking or other uses.

Union (YOON-yun) Having to do with the Northern states that stayed with the national government during the Civil War.

victory (VIK-tuh-ree) The winning of a battle.

volunteers (vah-lun-TEERZ) Soldiers who had jobs outside the military before the war.

INDEX

WEB SITES

Due to the changing nature of Internet links, the Rosen Publishing Group, Inc., has developed an online list of Web sites related to the subject of this book. This site is updated regularly. Please use this link to access the list:
www.powerkidslinks.com/jgb/lincoln/